Peekapoos

by Ruth Owen

PowerKiDS press™

New York

Published in 2015 by The Rosen Publishing Group, Inc.
29 East 21st Street, New York, NY 10010

First Edition

Produced for Rosen by Ruby Tuesday Books Ltd
Editor for Ruby Tuesday Books Ltd: Mark J. Sachner
US Editor: Joshua Shadowens
Designer: Emma Randall

Photo Credits:
Cover, 3, 4 (right), 23, 28–29, 30 © Superstock; 1, 5, 15 (top), 24–25 ©
Istockphoto; 4 (left), 4 (center), 6, 8–9, 11, 12–13, 14–15, 16–17, 18–19,
20–21 © Shutterstock; 7, 22 © Corbis; 10, 26–27 © Warren Photographic.

Library of Congress Cataloging-in-Publication Data

Owen, Ruth, 1967– author.
 Peekapoos / by Ruth Owen. — First edition.
    pages cm. -- (Designer dogs)
 Includes index.
 ISBN 978-1-4777-7031-3 (library binding) — ISBN 978-1-4777-7032-0 (pbk.) —
 ISBN 978-1-4777-7033-7 (6-pack)
 1. Peekapoo—Juvenile literature. 2. Toy dogs—Juvenile literature. 3. Dogs—
Juvenile literature. I. Title.
 SF429.P25O94 2015
 636.76—dc23
                                    2014004847

Manufactured in the United States of America

CPSIA Compliance Information: Batch #WS14PK8: For Further Information contact Rosen Publishing, New York, New York at 1-800-237-9932

Contents

woof

Meet a Peekapoo

What has soft, wavy hair, is loving and loyal, and can make a lot of noise? The answer is a peekapoo.

Peekapoos are **crossbreed** dogs. A crossbreed is a mixture of two different dog **breeds**. When a pekingese and a poodle have puppies together, they make peekapoos.

A peekapoo loves to be close to its human owners. It may only be a small dog, but it will be very protective of the people it loves!

Adult Pekingese

Adult poodle

Peekapoo puppy

Peekapoos are named after their parent breeds. The name "peekapoo" is made from the words "Pekingese" and "poodle."

Peekapoo puppies

People, Their Pups, and Peekapoos

Every breed of dog, even little peekapoos, has wild wolves as its **ancestors**. About 14,000 years ago, people began to train wolves and other wild dogs to be working animals and pets. People wanted dogs to do different jobs. So, over many years they **mated** different types of dogs together to create hundreds of different breeds.

Some dogs, such as border collies, were bred to herd sheep or cattle. Many breeds of small dogs were created to be **companion** dogs for people. The job of a peekapoo is to be a loving pet and companion.

A gray wolf

A border collie herding sheep

Small dog breeds, such as peekapoos, are often called lapdogs. That's because these dogs are small enough to sit on a person's lap. They are also happy to sit quietly for long periods of time on their owners' laps.

A peekapoo sitting on its owner's lap

What Are Designer Dogs?

Some breeds of dogs have been around for thousands of years. Designer dog breeds, such as peekapoos, are quite new breeds. Dog **breeders** only began breeding peekapoos about 50 years ago.

These new breeds of dogs are called designer dogs because dog breeders designed, or created, them from two older breeds. Some people, however, call these new dog breeds "designer dogs" because they believe the dogs are being bought as a fashion accessory—like a new designer handbag! People should never choose a dog breed just because it is fashionable and new.

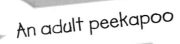

An adult peekapoo

A Pekingese

A designer dog, such as a peekapoo, might look like one of its parents more than the other. It might also look like a mixture of both its parents' breeds.

A poodle

Less "Ah-choo" with a Peekapoo

Millions of people would love to own a pet dog, but dogs make them ill. That's because these people have an **allergy** to dogs.

One of the problems is that dogs shed, or drop, lots of hair. The hair carries tiny pieces of dead skin called dander. When allergic people get near dog hair or dander, they may sneeze or struggle to breathe.

Poodle hair doesn't drop out, however, and it doesn't make allergic people ill. Crossbreed dogs that have a poodle parent often have this type of hair, too. This means that people with an allergy to dogs may not get sick when they are around a peekapoo.

A peekapoo puppy

There are several designer dog breeds that can be sneeze free because they have a poodle parent. These include labradoodles, goldendoodles, and cockapoos.

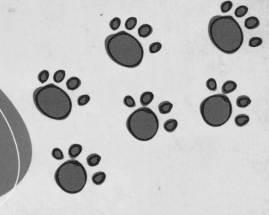

Golden retriever + poodle = goldendoodle

Cocker spaniel + poodle = cockapoo

Labrador retriever + poodle = labradoodle

Meet the Parents: Poodles

Poodles are extremely smart dogs that enjoy being taught new things and showing off their tricks. They form strong **bonds** with their owners.

A poodle's hair can be black, brown, gray, red, apricot, cream, white, or silver. The hair feels soft and woolly.

Some poodles are big, and some are very small. In fact, this dog breed comes in three sizes, standard (large), miniature, and **toy**. Peekapoos usually have a miniature or toy poodle as a parent.

Adult standard poodle size

Black coat

Height to shoulder = 15 inches (38 cm) or more

Adult miniature poodle size

Height to shoulder =
10 to 15 inches (25–38 cm)

Some poodle owners allow their dogs' hair to grow very long. Then the woolly, curly hair forms cords that look like dreadlocks!

White coat

Red coat

These white standard poodles have corded coats.

Adult toy poodle size

Height to shoulder:
about 10 inches
(25 cm)

13

Meet the Parents: Working Poodles

Peekapoos might be lapdogs, but their poodle parents were originally bred to be working dogs. They helped people hunt water birds, such as ducks. When a poodle's owner shot a duck, the dog's job was to dive into the pond or lake, pick up the dead bird, and carry it back to the hunter.

Today, most poodles no longer do this work. The water-loving pups still want to spend time in ponds, swimming pools, and the ocean, though. Poodles just love to play in water and are very good swimmers.

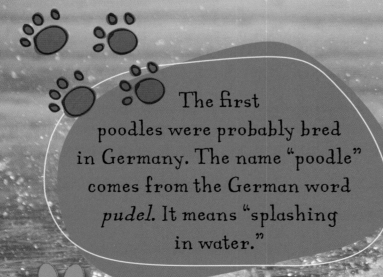

The first poodles were probably bred in Germany. The name "poodle" comes from the German word *pudel.* It means "splashing in water."

A poodle taking a bath

Meet the Parents: Pekingese

Pekingese may be small, but that doesn't stop them from feeling important and having lots of **dignity**.

A Pekingese's little body can be surprisingly heavy. That's because it is **stocky** and muscular. A full-grown Pekingese can weigh up to 14 pounds (6.4 kg).

Pekingese have an outer coat of long, rough hairs and a thick, soft undercoat. The hair forms a mane around the dog's head. A Pekingese may have hair that is white, red, black, brown, or a mixture of these colors.

Adult pekingese size

Height to shoulder = up to 9 inches (23 cm)

A Pekingese doesn't have a long muzzle like most dogs. If viewed from the side, its face is flat. It has a furry wrinkle of skin on its face that's shaped like an upside-down V.

17

Meet the Parents: A Pekingese Legend

There is a very old **legend** of how the Pekingese dog came to be. Once upon a time, a lion fell in love with a marmoset. The lion was huge, and the monkey was tiny. Their love could never be.

So the lion asked for help from the great spiritual leader Buddha. The lion asked that he be shrunk. He wanted, however, to keep his great lion spirit. The huge lion was made smaller and was able to be with his marmoset love. From this strange couple, so the legend says, came the Pekingese dog.

Lion

Golden lion tamarin marmoset

A Pekingese

Pekingese may be small, but they are brave. They will guard their toys and stand up for themselves against bigger dogs. People say they have the spirit of a lion!

19

Meet the Parents: Royal Pekingese

Pekingese have been around for centuries and are one of the world's oldest dog breeds. Ancient art from China includes pictures of Pekingese. The artworks are over 1,000 years old.

In China, Pekingese dogs were the treasured pets of emperors and empresses. No ordinary person was allowed to own one of these dogs. In fact, if a person stole a Pekingese from the royal family, that person would be put to death!

A Pekingese puppy

Pekingese dogs lived in palaces like this one in Beijing, China.

The Pekingese breed was named after China's ancient capital city, Peking. Today, Peking is called Beijing.

21

Peekapoo Looks

Just like their colorful parents, the coats of peekapoos can be many colors, including white, silver, gray, cream, apricot, chocolate-brown, red, and black. Their hair feels soft—a little like cotton balls.

Peekapoos come in a range of sizes, depending on the size of their parents. When fully grown, some peekapoos are very small and weigh only four pounds (1.8 kg). Larger peekapoos may weigh up to 20 pounds (9 kg).

Adult peekapoo size

Height to shoulder = up to 11 inches (28 cm)

If a peekapoo has a long coat, it should be brushed every day. If its hair is clipped, or cut, it should be brushed twice a week.

An apricot and a black peekapoo puppy

23

Perfect Peekapoo Pups

A peekapoo puppy may have a Pekingese mother and a poodle father, or the other way around.

The mother dog can give birth to up to eight peekapoo puppies at one time. The tiny newborn pups cannot walk, and their eyes are closed. They sleep cuddled up with their brothers and sisters. When they get hungry, they drink milk from their mom.

After about a week, the puppies' eyes open. By four weeks old, they are walking and playing.

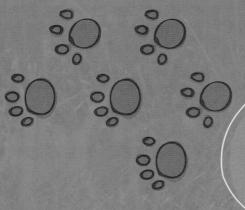

When it is about four weeks old, a peekapoo pup will start to try out doggie skills such as wagging its tail and barking.

Peekapoo Personalities

A peekapoo is a gentle, loving dog that will happily spend its days cuddled up to its owner.

Peekapoos can be unsure about meeting new people and other animals, though. Therefore, it's very important that peekapoo puppies are well socialized. This means they are given the chance to spend time with other pets and different people while they are young. Then they learn not to be afraid or shy, and will enjoy making new friends when they are older.

A shy peekapoo puppy checks out a possible new friend.

Peekapoos are bred to be companion dogs. If they are left on their own for long periods of time, they miss their owners and become very unhappy.

Everything checked out OK, so now it's best friends forever!

Peekapoos on Guard

A peekapoo may be a lapdog, but it still has lots of energy. It needs at least one walk and an energetic play session every day.

Just like its Pekingese parent, a peekapoo has the spirit of a lion! These little dogs are very protective of their human family. They may be small, but they have very big barks, and they aren't shy about using them. If they hear a strange noise or a stranger comes to the house, they will bark loudly and a lot. This means a peekapoo is a very good watchdog.

A peekapoo may live for up to 15 years.

Glossary

allergy (A-lur-jee)
When a person's body reacts badly to something such as an animal or type of food. An allergy may make a person sneeze, get sore skin, vomit, or become seriously ill.

ancestors
(AN-ses-terz) Relatives who lived long ago.

bonds (BONDZ)
Close connections based on love and trust.

breeders (BREE-derz)
People who breed animals, such as dogs, and sell them.

breeds (BREEDZ)
Different types of dogs. The word "breed" is also used to describe the act of mating two dogs in order for them to have puppies.

companion
(kum-PAN-yun)
A person or animal with whom one spends a lot of time.

crossbreed (KROS-breed)
A type of dog created
from two different breeds.

dignity (DIG-nuh-tee)
Acting in a calm, serious
way that deserves respect.

legend (LEH-jend)
A story handed down
over the years that may
sometimes be based on
some facts but cannot
be proved to be true.

mated (MAYT-ed)
Brought together a male
and a female animal so
that they would mate
and produce young.

stocky (STO-kee)
Solid and well built.

toy (TOY)
The word used to describe
the size of a dog that is
very small.

Websites
Due to the changing nature
of Internet links, PowerKids Press has
developed an online list of websites related to the
subject of this book. This site is updated regularly.
Please use this link to access the list:

www.powerkidslinks.com/ddog/peek/

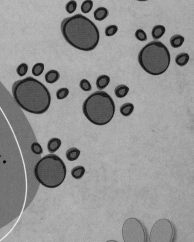

Read More

Gagne, Tammy. *Poodles.* All About Dogs. Mankato, MN: Capstone Press, 2010.

Heneghan, Judith. *Love Your Dog.* Your Perfect Pet. New York: Windmill Books, 2013.

Walker, Kathryn. *See How Dogs Grow.* See How They Grow. New York: PowerKids Press, 2009.

Index

MARY

MARK

Author's Note

*This story is based on various versions of the Karuk myth.
The Karuk – meaning "upriver" – people are native to
the rugged Klamath River region of Northwest California.
With their neighbors the Yurok, Hupa, and Shasta, they
share many of the old stories. This is one.*

Text Copyright © 1993 by Jonathan London.
Illustrations copyright © 1993 by Sylvia Long.
Afterword Copyright © 1993 by Julian Lang.
All rights reserved.

Book design by Alison K. Berry.
Printed in Hong Kong.

Library of Congress Cataloging-in-Publication Data
  London, Jonathan, 1947 -
  Fire Race: a Karuk coyote tale about how fire
  came to the people / by Jonathan London and
  Lanny Pinola; with an afterword by Julian Lang;
  illustrated by Sylvia Long.
  Summary: With the help of other animals, Wise
  Old Coyote manages to acquire fire from the
  wicked Yellow Jacket sisters.
  ISBN 0-8118-0241-8
  1. Karuk Indians–Legends. 2. Coyote (Legendary
  Character)–Legends. 3. Fire–Folklore. [1. Karuk
  Indians–Legends. 2. Indians of North America–
  California–Legends. 3. Fire–Folklore. 4. Coyote
  (Legendary Character)]
  I. Pinola, Lanny. II. Long, Sylvia, ill. III. Title.
  E99.k25L65 1993   92-32352
  398.24'52974442–dc20   CIP
                                AC

Distributed in Canada by Raincoast Books
112 East Third Avenue, Vancouver, B.C. V5T 1C8

10 9 8 7 6 5 4 3 2

Chronicle Books
275 Fifth Street
San Francisco, California 94103

*To the People who loved these stories, made them
come alive, and passed them on.*

*With thanks to Ricardo Sierra, from whom I first heard a
version of this story; to Sue Plummer, Sebastopol's children's
librarian; to Joe Bruchac, Abenaki storyteller; and to
Linda Vit, Karuk artist.*
– Jonathan London

*For my parents with love and thanks for their wisdom,
encouragement and kindness. Their joy in each other and
the natural world around them is a continuing source of
pleasure and inspiration for their children.*
– Sylvia Long

*To my grandmother, Elizabeth Conrad, who first told me
this story and many more; to Jubilee, my son, and to Lisa.*
– Julian Lang

FIRE RACE

A Karuk Coyote Tale About How Fire Came to the People

retold by Jonathan London with Lanny Pinola

illustrated by Sylvia Long

with an afterword by Julian Lang

CHRONICLE BOOKS · SAN FRANCISCO

Long ago, the animal people had no fire. Day and night, they huddled in their houses in the dark, and ate their food uncooked. In the winter, they were so cold, icicles hung from their fur. Oh, they were miserable!

Then one day, Wise Old Coyote gathered everybody together. "We have heard about fire," he said. "But the only fire is far upriver, at the world's end. It's guarded by the Yellow Jacket sisters high atop a snowy mountain. They are wicked, and will not share it. But listen, if we all cooperate and work together, we can steal the fire." There was much fearful murmuring about the Yellow Jacket sisters, but all grew quiet as Coyote told them his plan. Then he went on his way.

Grandfather Coyote slowly trudged up the mountain at the world's end. When at last he came to the Yellow Jacket's house, smoke was rising from the smokehole.

Coyote looked inside. The three old sisters were sitting around the fire.
Coyote said, as friendly as can be, "If you let me in, I'll make you all look pretty."
Suspicious, the three sisters put their heads close together and buzzed.
"Come in," they said. "But no tricks!"

Old Man Coyote sat down and took a chunk of oak bark between his toes and held it in the fire. When it had burned into a blackened coal, he marked their yellow faces and bodies with black stripes to make them pretty. "Now," said Coyote, "if you close your eyes, I will make you even prettier."

Here was Coyote's chance! While the Yellow Jackets' eyes were closed, he took the charred oak in his teeth, and silent as the moon in the sky, he crept outside. Then he raced down the mountain like the wind.

When the Yellow Jacket sisters found out that Coyote had tricked them, they were screaming mad. They, too, flew like the wind. And it wasn't long until they caught up to Coyote.

They were almost on him when Coyote tripped, rolled downhill like a
snowball, and landed smack at Eagle's feet. Snatching the glowing coal in
his talons, Eagle spread his wings and took to the sky.

Eagle was swift, but the Yellow Jackets soon caught up with him. Suddenly, Eagle dropped the coal. Below, Mountain Lion caught it in his great teeth, and bounded off through the snow. Still, the furious Yellow Jackets followed.

Just as they were about to sting Mountain Lion, Fox snatched the fiery coal, and bounced in among the tall cedar and pine. Fox ran and ran, until she was so tired, she couldn't take another step. She huffed and huffed. Her breath made clouds, and the Yellow Jackets were right behind her.

Just in time, Bear took the fire and lunged away through some brambles.

Bear, too, was quick, yet the Yellow Jackets were right on top of her.

Even Bear could not fight them off, and she finally tumbled in exhaustion.

As Bear fell, Measuring Worm, the Long One, took the fire. The Long One stretched way out over three ridges, yet the Yellow Jackets were there, waiting, ready to strike.

Somehow, right under the Yellow Jackets's eyes, Turtle sneaked in, grabbed the fire, and scrambled off. But of course Turtle was slow, and one of the Yellow Jacket sisters stung him in his tail. *Akee! Akee! Akee!*

Turtle pulled in his head and legs and flip-flopped down the hill. *Fallumph.*
Fallumph. Fallumph. The Yellow Jackets were swarming all over Turtle, when
Frog leaped out of the river and swallowed the fire. *Gulp!*

Then Frog hopped back into the river – *plop* – and sat on the bottom. The Yellow Jackets stormed the river, circling once, circling twice, circling three times, buzzing the surface. They waited and they waited and they waited, but Frog held the fire, and his breath. Finally, the Yellow Jackets gave up, and flew back home.

As soon as the Yellow Jacket sisters were gone, Frog burst out of the water,
and spat the hot coal into the roots of a willow growing along the river.
The tree swallowed the fire, and the animal people didn't know what to do.

Then once again Coyote came along, and the animal people said, "Grandfather, you must show us how to get the fire from the willow." So Old Man Coyote, who is very wise and knows these things, said, "Hah!" and he showed them how to rub two willow sticks together over dry moss to make fire.

From that time on the people have known how to coax fire from the wood in order to keep warm and to cook their food. And at night in the seasons of cold, they have sat in a circle around their fires and listened as the elders told the old stories. And so it is, even to this day. *Kupanakanakana.*

AFTERWORD

Ishpukatunvêech iikiv
a "little money" necklace

Storytelling is very important for the Karuk people. Both children and adults are taught through stories about the special relationship that we must keep between ourselves and the natural world. The Karuk people are Fix the Earth People. Many of us gather each year to clean special ceremonial places, to pray for water food and earth food. We pray so the children and elders will be healthy. We ask that the natural world around us become stable and remain balanced.

Traditional stories describe the natural world and human nature. In *Fire Race,* we are reminded just how important the willow tree is to our way of life. We are told of one way that Coyote helped us (he most often fooled people and caused great calamity). We are reminded that we must remember and respect each other. The story reveals that all natural living things are important, from the little frog to the soaring eagle.

Today, many Karuk children are told this story in their native language. Often stories contain ancient songs and funny jokes. Stories like *Fire Race* help the Karuk people love themselves. The stories are called *pikva* and are most often told during the winter months. During the spring, summer, and fall, we see all the animals and places that were spoken of in the stories. This, then, is wisdom from the Karuk people: the land, the people and the animals are all related.
Yootva!

– Julian Lang

BIBLIOGRAPHY

KAROK MYTHS by A.L. Kroeber and E.W. Gifford (University of California Press; most notably the stories told by Little Ike in 1902 and Mary Ike in 1940)

GIVING BIRTH TO THUNDER, SLEEPING WITH HIS DAUGHTER by Barry Lopez (Andrews & McNeel, Inc., 1977)

KARUK: THE UPRIVER PEOPLE by Maureen Bell (Naturegraph Publishers, 1991)

TO THE AMERICAN INDIAN: REMINISCENCES OF A YUROK WOMAN by Lucy Thompson (Heyday Books, 1991; original copyright 1916)

THE HOVER COLLECTION OF KARUK BASKETS by the Clarke Memorial Musuem/Eureka, California (1985)

DAWN OF THE WORLD: COAST MIWOK MYTHS by Hart Merrian, ed. by Bonni Peterson (1976)

THE MAIDU INDIAN MYTHS AND STORIES OF HANC'IBYJIM ed. and trans. by William Shipley (Heyday Books, 1991)

COYOTE WAS GOING THERE by Jerry Ramsey (Washington University Press, 1977)

THE EARTH IS OUR MOTHER: A GUIDE TO THE INDIANS OF CALIFORNIA by Dolan Eargle, Jr. (Tree's Company Press, 1986, 1991)

KEEPERS OF THE ANIMALS: NATIVE AMERICAN STORIES AND WILDLIFE ACTIVITIES FOR CHILDREN by Michael J. Caduto and Joseph Bruchac (Fulcrum, 1991)

Yuxchananach iikiv
abalone chip necklace

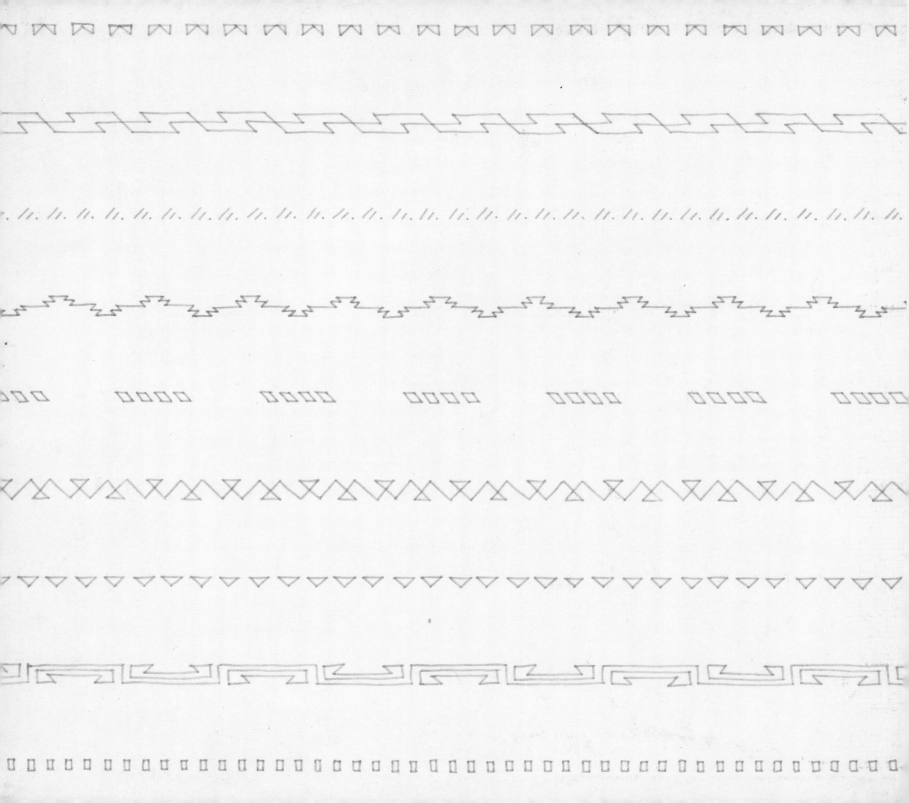